BRITANNICA BEGINNER BIOS

# LAURA INGALLS WILDER
## CHILDREN'S AUTHOR

CORONA BREZINA

**Britannica**
Educational Publishing

IN ASSOCIATION WITH

**ROSEN**
EDUCATIONAL SERVICES

Published in 2018 by Britannica Educational Publishing (a trademark of Encyclopædia Britannica, Inc.) in association with The Rosen Publishing Group, Inc.
29 East 21st Street, New York, NY 10010

Distributed exclusively by Rosen Publishing.
To see additional Britannica Educational Publishing titles, go to rosenpublishing.com.

First Edition

**Britannica Educational Publishing**
J.E. Luebering: Executive Director, Core Editorial
Mary Rose McCudden: Editor, Britannica Student Encyclopedia

**Rosen Publishing**
Kathy Kuhtz Campbell: Senior Editor
Nelson Sá: Art Director
Brian Garvey: Series Designer
Ellina Litmanovich: Book Layout
Cindy Reiman: Photography Manager
Nicole DiMella: Photo Researcher

**Library of Congress Cataloging-in-Publication Data**

Names: Brezina, Corona, author.
Title: Laura Ingalls Wilder : children's author / Corona Brezina.
Description: New York : Britannica Educational Publishing, in Association with Rosen Educational Services, 2018. | Series: Britannica beginner bios | Includes bibliographical references and index. | Audience: Grades 1–4.
Identifiers: LCCN 2017015879| ISBN 9781680488180 (library bound) | ISBN 9781680488173 (pbk.) | ISBN 9781538300244 (6 pack)
Subjects: LCSH: Wilder, Laura Ingalls, 1867–1957—Juvenile literature. | Authors, American—20th century—Biography—Juvenile literature. | Women pioneers—United States—Biography—Juvenile literature.
Classification: LCC PS3545.I342 Z58 2018 | DDC 813/.52 [B] —dc23
LC record available at https://lccn.loc.gov/2017015879

*Manufactured in the United States of America*

# CONTENTS

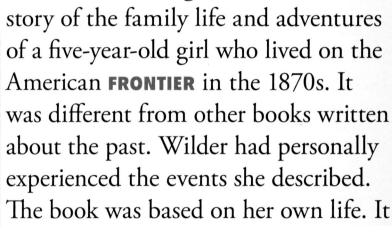

# CHAPTER ONE

# TALES FROM THE PRAIRIE

In 1932, Laura Ingalls Wilder published a children's book called *Little House in the Big Woods*. It told the story of the family life and adventures of a five-year-old girl who lived on the American **FRONTIER** in the 1870s. It was different from other books written about the past. Wilder had personally experienced the events she described. The book was based on her own life. It

Laura Ingalls Wilder is shown in a photograph taken when she was about fifty years old, while she was writing for a weekly farm magazine.

4

is not considered an autobiography, though. An autobiography is a history of a person's life, written by that person. Wilder changed around some facts when she wrote her stories.

Readers loved Wilder's account of the joys and challenges of frontier life. Her descriptions of old-fashioned everyday routines as the seasons changed made kids feel like

An illustration from 1867 shows a common pioneer's home on the Western frontier—the log cabin and covered wagon would have been familiar to Laura. A covered wagon is a horse-drawn wagon with an arched canvas top.

## Vocabulary

The FRONTIER is a region at the edge of settled land in a country.

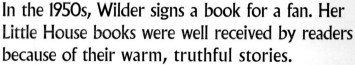

In the 1950s, Wilder signs a book for a fan. Her Little House books were well received by readers because of their warm, truthful stories.

like they were growing up alongside Laura. In time, Wilder continued her story in a sequel called *Little House on the Prairie*. *Little House on the Prairie* is the most famous of all her books.

Over the next few years, the series grew to a total of eight books. They describe how Wilder's family moved often. Her family and friends experienced hardships and successes. By the end of the

**Quick Fact**

The American Library Association has an award called the Laura Ingalls Wilder Award. It was established to honor American authors or illustrators who have made a lasting contribution to children's literature. Wilder was the first recipient of the medal, in 1954.

series, the little girl from the Big Woods married and moved into her own house.

Wilder's stories provide a firsthand view of a time of change in American history. Today, the Little House books are considered classics of children's literature. Young readers continue to relate to and be inspired by Wilder's descriptions of the American spirit and independence on the frontier.

# CHAPTER TWO

# A FAMILY OF PIONEERS

Laura was born on February 7, 1867, near Pepin, Wisconsin. Her parents were Charles and Caroline Ingalls, whom she called Ma and Pa in her books. Laura had a sister, Mary, who was two years older. The Ingalls

During Laura's early years, the Ingalls family lived in a log cabin in the woods near Pepin, Wisconsin (a replica is shown here).

family lived in a log cabin in the woods far away from any neighbors. Many members of Laura's extended family also lived in the area.

In 1869, the Ingalls family moved to "Indian Territory" in Kansas. There they were **PIONEERS**. During this period of history, the United States was taking over land to the west that was occupied by Native Americans. The government did this through agreements, land sales, and military force. Many American

Pioneers are shown traveling westward over the plains in covered wagons. A pair of horses named Pet and Patty pulled the Ingallses' covered wagon.

American settlers, including Laura's family, saw this territory as an opportunity to start a new life on the Western frontier. Laura was just a toddler during the family's years in Kansas, although the "Laura" in *Little House on the Prairie* is five years old.

The Ingalls family made the long journey from Wisconsin in a covered wagon pulled by horses. Once they arrived, Pa built a one-room log cabin. The family experienced many hardships and dangers in Kansas. Laura later remembered looking out of the window one night and seeing the house surrounded by howling wolves. When summer arrived, everyone in the family fell ill to a disease that was probably malaria, which is

## Quick Fact

Later in her life, Laura said that she spent more time researching *Little House on the Prairie* than any other book because she was too young to remember many details.

caused by mosquito bites. Another time, a prairie fire came close to burning down the cabin.

Laura was frightened of the Native Americans, with their unfamiliar appearance and customs. The Native

Tensions and even conflicts sometimes arose between newly arrived settlers and Native Americans, as Laura described in *Little House on the Prairie.*

Americans disliked the American settlers, too, for taking their land. The authorities feared that fighting could break out between the two groups.

In 1871, the Ingalls family packed up to go back to Wisconsin. The family had grown during their time in Kansas. Laura's younger sister, Carrie, was born in 1870.

The Ingalls family moved back into their old house in the Wisconsin woods. They returned to

Laura and her sisters helped their mother with the housework, which included tasks such as cleaning, churning butter, baking, and mending clothes.

familiar routines of raising crops, preserving food, and getting together with family for special occasions. Pa hunted, fished, and trapped animals such as mink and foxes. The girls helped with housework, and Laura and Mary both started attending school. At night, Pa would play songs on his fiddle and tell stories about his family and childhood.

# CHAPTER THREE

# GROWING UP ON THE FRONTIER

Laura's family moved many times during her childhood and teenage years. Pa was always ready for adventures and new opportunities. But frontier life could be cruel. The family was sometimes forced to move because of hardships experienced in their new home.

In 1873, the Ingalls family left Wisconsin and set out for the frontier again. This time, they moved west to Minnesota. They departed during the winter and spent several months in a deserted cabin as they waited for spring. Then they continued their journey and reached a small prairie town called Walnut Grove.

A modern replica of the Ingalls family's sod dugout on Plum Creek shows how the one-room house had thick earth walls and a roof covered by grass.

Laura's family settled on a homestead next to a stream called Plum Creek. They lived in a sod dugout house built by an earlier owner. Later, Pa built a house made of lumber. Their field of wheat grew tall.

But the years at Plum Creek were difficult for the family. A swarm of grasshoppers destroyed their wheat crop. Pa was forced to leave the family to earn money in the East. The next year, the grasshoppers returned. The family decided to move to Iowa, where a friend wanted Pa to help manage a hotel. In 1875, Ma had given birth to a baby boy named Charles Frederick. Sadly, he died in 1876 during the journey to Iowa.

Laura and her family briefly lived in the Burr Oak House, also called the Masters Hotel, in Iowa while Laura's father helped manage the hotel. They lived there from 1876 to 1877.

The Ingalls family spent a year living in Burr Oak, Iowa. There, another little sister, Grace, was born in 1877. In the Little House series, Laura did not mention this period spent in a town. In 1877, they returned to Walnut Grove. For Laura, it felt like she was coming home. She was outstanding in school and worked in a hotel in the summer. Tragedy struck the family in 1879, though, when Mary grew gravely ill. She got better, but she was blind for the rest of her life.

Later in 1879, the Ingalls family set out for the Dakota Territory. Pa had been offered work by the railroad.

Laura (*right*) is shown here with her younger sister Carrie (*left*) and her older sister Mary (*middle*).

He ran a store for railroad workers and later took on other jobs for the railroad. The family settled down for good in De Smet, part of what is now South Dakota. Later, in *The Long Winter*, Laura would describe the winter of 1880–81. It was so harsh that people would remember that winter for years

**Quick Fact**

afterward. For seven months beginning in October, frequent **BLIZZARDS** would blow in thick drifts of snow. It was bitterly cold. Food and fuel began to run low in town. Finally, in May, the first train of the year arrived with supplies.

After living in at least a dozen different homes during Laura's early years, the Ingalls family finally settled down in De Smet, now in South Dakota, in 1879.

Ma valued education very highly. The family saved up money to send Mary away to study at the Iowa College for the Blind. Mary left home in late 1881 and graduated in 1889.

Meanwhile, Laura became a teacher at a young age. She later described how she took the teacher's exam and received her certificate when she was just

**Vocabulary**

**BLIZZARDS** are severe winter storms often accompanied by blinding snow and wind.

During her time at the Iowa College for the Blind, Mary Ingalls studied traditional academic subjects as well as music and sewing.

fifteen years old. Qualified teachers were scarce, so Laura was allowed to become a teacher in spite of being underage.

In 1882 Laura accepted the first of many teaching jobs. For two months in the winter, she taught at a school outside De Smet and boarded with a family on a nearby homestead. Then she returned home and went back to school as a student. Later, she held other teaching jobs closer to town. Still, Laura herself never graduated from high school.

# CHAPTER FOUR

# MANLY AND LAURA

Shortly before she began teaching, Laura met Almanzo Wilder. She called him "Manly" and he called her "Bessie," because he had a sister named Laura.

Laura described Manly's early life in *Farmer Boy*, the second book in the Little House series. He grew up on a farm in Malone,

Ten years older than Laura, Almanzo Wilder was skilled at handling horses and took Laura on long drives across the prairie in his buggy.

19

A farmer rides his horse during the early stages of a blizzard in South Dakota. Manly and a friend made a trip in a blizzard to buy some wheat for the people in De Smet who were running out of food.

New York. In 1879, he set out for the Dakota Territory, along with a brother, Royal, and a sister, Eliza. Laura considered the Wilders to be well-off compared to her own family.

During the long winter, Manly and a friend became known as heroes to the townspeople of De Smet. As food ran low, they volunteered to travel with horses and a sled to a farm outside town to buy some wheat. A blizzard struck after they departed, but they managed to complete the trip and return with bushels of wheat.

Laura first became acquainted with Manly one Sunday when he asked to see her home from church. While she lived away from home during her teaching job, Manly would pick her up on Friday to take her to her parents' home in a sleigh pulled by horses. Manly courted Laura over the next few years. He took her on **BUGGY** rides and to events such as ice cream socials and dances. During one buggy ride, Manly asked Laura if she would accept an engagement ring from him. She said yes.

Laura and Manly were married in 1885 in

During the winter that she lived away from home, Manly took Laura back to her parents' house on Fridays in his sleigh.

Vocabulary

A **BUGGY** is a light horse-drawn carriage that generally holds one or two people.

the preacher's house. They settled down on Manly's homestead, which was about one mile (1.6 kilometers) outside De Smet. Their daughter, Rose, was born in 1886. They named her for the roses that grew on their prairie.

The Wilders' first few years together brought many hardships and sorrows. Their crops failed to thrive because of drought, hail, and other weather events. As a result, they were unable to pay their debts. They were forced to sell or rent out some of

## Quick Fact

The Little House series originally ended with Manly and Laura's wedding. Wilder began writing an account of her early married years, but she never finished it. The final book, *The First Four Years*, was published from this draft many years after her death.

their land. Then in 1888, they were both stricken by diphtheria, an infection that affects the nose and throat. In very bad cases, it can cause serious problems. Wilder recovered fully, but Manly's legs were partly paralyzed. He needed to walk with a cane for the rest of his life.

In 1889, the Wilders had an infant son, but the boy lived for less than a month. Not long afterward, a fire destroyed their house and almost everything they owned.

The Wilders gave up their land. They stayed with Manly's parents for a time, then briefly moved to Florida for Manly's health. Next, the family returned to De Smet, where they lived in a house in town. In 1894, the Wilders moved to Missouri, where they would live for the rest of their lives.

# CHAPTER FIVE

# SHARING THE LITTLE HOUSE STORIES

Wilder called her Missouri home Rocky Ridge Farm. The Wilders finally made a success of farming, raising horses and chickens and other farm animals. In 1911, a newspaper **EDITOR** contacted Wilder inviting her to send in an article. Wilder became a regular writer of a newspaper column for the *Missouri Ruralist*.

**Vocabulary**

An **EDITOR** is a person whose job is to correct, revise, and prepare a work for publication.

Wilder lived for more than sixty years at Rocky Ridge Farm in Missouri, where she and her husband raised Morgan horses and other livestock.

Her daughter, Rose, also became a successful writer and journalist. In 1915, Wilder took a trip to visit her in San Francisco, California, where Rose was a reporter for the *San Francisco Bulletin*.

Wilder's only child, Rose Wilder Lane, established a successful career as a writer and traveled throughout Europe, the Middle East, and Asia.

After Wilder's newspaper days were behind her, she decided to write her autobiography. Her daughter encouraged her and helped edit her writing. In 1930, Rose sent her mother's manuscript, *Pioneer Girl*, to a publisher. One day, a children's department editor expressed interest in a version of Laura's childhood experiences. Parts of *Pioneer Girl* were reworked to become *Little House in the Big Woods*, which came out in 1932. Seven more books of the series followed over the next twelve years. Wilder became a famous and beloved author. She received lots of fan mail. Wilder died at her Missouri home in 1957.

A version of *Pioneer Girl* was finally published in 2014. Readers could now compare the fact-based autobiography with the made-up parts of the children's books. Wilder had changed some details about characters and events. She left out some of the difficult parts of her life, such as the death of her baby brother and an episode when Ma was very ill. She also avoided some of the occurrences that probably frightened her as a child. These included a time when she was nearly attacked and the extent that the family suffered because of money troubles.

The second illustrator for the Little House books, Garth Williams, visited some sites from Laura's childhood so that his drawings would be accurate.

**Quick Fact**

Several of the Little House books were recognized as Newbery Honor books on their publication. The Newbery Medal is one of the highest awards in children's literature.

Wilder's books are now considered classics of children's literature. They continue to bring the pioneer period to life for new generations of American children. The book series also inspired a popular TV series. The Rocky Ridge Farm in Missouri is now a museum, and other locations important in Laura's life have been protected as historical sites. Every year, many fans of the Little House books visit these sites to feel connected to Laura and the life she shared with her readers all around the world.

# TIMELINE

**1867:** Laura Elizabeth Ingalls is born on February 7 in Wisconsin.

**1869:** The Ingalls family moves to "Indian Territory" in Kansas.

**1871:** The family returns to Wisconsin.

**1874:** The Ingalls family settles in Walnut Grove, Minnesota.

**1876:** The family moves to Burr Oak, Iowa.

**1877:** The Ingalls family returns to Walnut Grove.

**1879:** The family leaves Minnesota and settles in the Dakota Territory, near the town of De Smet. The site is now in South Dakota.

**1880–81:** The town of De Smet faces the harsh "long winter."

**1882:** Laura receives her teaching certificate.

**1885:** Laura and Almanzo Wilder are married in De Smet.

**1886:** Rose Wilder is born in De Smet.

**1888:** Laura and Manly get diphtheria.

**1889:** The Wilders' house burns down in a fire.

**1890:** The Wilders leave De Smet.

**1894:** The Wilders move to Rocky Ridge Farm in Mansfield, Missouri.

**1911:** Laura begins writing for the *Missouri Ruralist*.

**1932:** *Little House in the Big Woods* is published.

**1935:** *Little House on the Prairie* is published.

**1949:** Almanzo Wilder dies in Missouri.

**1954:** Laura is honored with the first Laura Ingalls Library Award.

**1957:** Laura dies at Rocky Ridge Farm on February 10.

**2014:** *Pioneer Girl*, Wilder's autobiography, is published.

# GLOSSARY

**CHALLENGE** A difficult task or problem.

**CLASSIC** Notable as one of the best of its kind.

**COURT** To engage in a social relationship usually leading to marriage.

**DIPHTHERIA** A serious disease that makes breathing very difficult.

**EXTENDED FAMILY** A family that includes not only parents and children but also other relatives, such as grandparents, aunts, or uncles.

**HARDSHIP** Something that causes pain or loss.

**HOMESTEAD** A home and surrounding land.

**JOURNALIST** An editor of or writer for a newspaper, magazine, radio, or television news.

**MALARIA** A serious disease that causes chills and fever. It is passed from one person to another by mosquito bites.

**MANUSCRIPT** A written composition or document.

**MEASLES** A spreadable disease that causes a fever and red spots on the skin.

**PARALYZE** To make someone unable to move or feel all or part of the body.

**PRESERVE** To prepare vegetables, fruits, or meats to be kept for future use.

**SCARLET FEVER** A very serious and spreadable disease that causes a fever, sore throat, and a red rash.

**SEQUEL** A book that continues a story begun in another.

**SLEIGH** An open, usually horse-drawn, vehicle with runners for use on snow or ice.

**TERRITORY** A geographic area belonging to or under the control of a government.

# FOR MORE INFORMATION

# BOOKS

Collins, Carolyn Strom, and Christina Wyss Eriksson. *The World of Little House*. Rev. ed. New York, NY: Harper, 2015.

Wilder, Laura Ingalls. *By the Shores of Silver Lake*. New York, NY: HarperCollins, 2008.

Wilder, Laura Ingalls. *Farmer Boy*. Rev. ed. New York, NY: HarperCollins, 2017.

Wilder, Laura Ingalls. *Little House in the Big Woods*. Rev ed. New York, NY: HarperCollins, 2017.

Wilder, Laura Ingalls. *Little House on the Prairie*. Rev. ed. New York, NY: HarperCollins, 2017.

Wilder, Laura Ingalls. *Little Town on the Prairie*. New York, NY: HarperCollins, 2007.

Wilder, Laura Ingalls. *The Long Winter*. Rev. ed. New York, NY: HarperCollins, 2011.

Wilder, Laura Ingalls. *On the Banks of Plum Creek*. Rev. ed. New York, NY: HarperCollins, 2008.

Wilder, Laura Ingalls. *These Happy Golden Years*. New York, NY: HarperCollins, 2008.

# WEBSITES

Because of the changing nature of internet links, Rosen Publishing has developed an online list of websites related to the subject of this book. This site is updated regularly. Please use this link to access the list:

http://www.rosenlinks.com/BBB/wilder

# INDEX